# _All About the Werewolf_

There's a Werewolf in my Class #2

Written by Ann Thornton

Illustrated by Daniel Naranjo

# DEDICATION

To my youngest.

Your imagination and love of all

things Pokemon provided tons

of inspiration for this book.

## ACKNOWLEDGEMENTS

Thank you to WonderDesign11 for the fantastic pictures. To my own children who beta read and gave suggestions. And to all the online groups who help indie authors such as myself learn and grow in order to put our work into the world.

## NEWSLETTER

Join my newsletter and stay up to date on all my newest releases and receive 3 free coloring pages for immediate download! Visit

annthornton.com

to sign up, purchase signed paperbacks or contact me to do a presentation at your local school!

# CHAPTER 1

"Dude…" Silas grunted as Axel climbed over his head in order to get to the bus window. "Move over!"

"You move over!" Axel shot back. He grinned when he finally was able to let his tongue hang out in the wind.

Silas laughed and switched places with his friend. A friend who just happened to be a werewolf. Axel sometimes acted more like a dog than a person, but that was part of what made him so fun.

Silas looked around his seat to see Declan, his other best friend, with his Pokemon cards spread out on the seat. "What's up?" Silas asked.

Declan glanced at Silas, shrugged, and went back to the cards.

Declan didn't talk much, but Silas didn't mind. They had been friends since they were little kids. Now they were in fourth grade and still did everything together.

"Got anything new?" Silas asked. Declan loved Pokemon cards and was constantly working his way through them. Silas had a few, but he was

interested in other games instead of Pokemon.

Declan shook his head.

"Did Mr. Parker give your class that geography assignment?" Silas asked. "Where you have to build a diorama thingie?"

"Oh, man," Axel groaned from his place at the window. "I got assigned the Mayan people." He scrunched his nose at Silas. "I'm gonna have to build a home out of toothpicks or something."

"Toothpicks!" Silas exclaimed. "That's gonna take forever!"

Axel nodded. "I know."

The bus came to a stop and soon all the students were scrambling down the steps to the elementary school. Someone pushed Silas's shoulder and he glared back to see his sister, Sarah, smirking.

"Watch it," she said with a smile.

Silas rolled his eyes. He didn't always get along with his sister, but he knew she was only teasing him. "You watch it," he shot back. Gripping his backpack tighter, he hurried to catch up with Axel and Declan.

"Hey, Dog Boy!"

Silas frowned. That was a nickname that the kids had given Axel when he moved to their town. At first nobody had wanted to be Axel's friend, but when they discovered how good he was at sports, soon everyone wanted to be around Axel.

Luckily, Silas and Declan were Axel's best friends. In fact, they had formed the HOWL club. Right now it was just the three of them, but someday they might let others in.

"Don't call him that," Silas said as he ran up to Axel's shoulder.

Axel waved a hand in the air. "It's okay, Si. It doesn't bother me." Axel stepped forward to the fifth-grader who had spoken and they exchanged a complicated handshake.

Silas frowned and looked at Declan, who shrugged. After the fifth-grader had left, Silas turned to Axel. "I didn't know you were friends with him."

Axel smiled. "Yeah. He was in the soccer game last week. Didn't you see him?"

Silas kicked at the ground. "Nah." Truth was, Silas hadn't played last week. Their fourth-grade team had too many players and Silas had been chosen to sit out. Usually he played goalie, but now that Axel was here, they didn't need Silas as much.

It had hurt, but Silas tried not to care. Axel was really good, so it was better for him to be the one playing. With the werewolf on their team, the fourth-graders had even beat the fifth-graders twice now. It was something they had only dreamed about before.

"Oh," Axel said, frowning. "Well, he was there and he talked to me before recess was over." Axel beamed. "He said I had good skills. He wants me to try out for the league team this summer."

Silas nodded. "Cool." He smiled at Axel, but inside, Silas felt a little bit upset. He loved to play soccer and other sports and had been playing for a long time. Axel had only moved into their town a couple of months ago and already the older kids were picking him for their team. Silas would love to play on the league team, but he'd never been invited.

The bell rang and all three boys looked toward the school. "Guess we gotta go inside," Axel said.

Declan grunted and began walking.

"Come on, buddy!" Axel called to Silas.

Silas smiled. Being called Axel's friend made him feel special and he decided he didn't care if Axel was better at soccer. They were buddies, and that was enough.

# CHAPTER 2

"Axel!" Finley shouted. "Pass it over here!"

Silas watched as Axel nodded and began to steer the ball toward Finley's side of the field.

"I think maybe you should take a nap," Chloe teased Silas.

He finally got to play today, but the ball had only been down to his side of the field twice. Axel and Finley always seemed to be able to kick it back to the fifth-grader's side.

Silas gave Chloe a glare. "I need to be ready," he said angrily.

Chloe shrugged. "If the ball ever makes it back. It seems like Finley and Axel make up our whole team." She plopped onto the grass and began to pick at the blades.

Silas knew exactly what she meant. Finley used to be the best player in their grade. In fact, he had played with the older kids before Axel showed up. But now that Axel was here, Finley wanted to play with him.

"Everybody wants to play with him," Silas grumbled to himself, kicking at the grass.

"SILAS!"

Silas jerked his head up just in time to duck as the ball whizzed into the net.

"What are you doing?" Finley cried, waving his hands in the air.

Silas felt his cheeks grow hot and he clenched his fists in anger. The one time he hadn't been paying attention, and the ball got past him. He couldn't tell if he was more angry or embarrassed.

The bell rang before anyone could say anything else. They all headed back into the school.

"Hey," Axel called out. He ran up to Silas and put his arm around his shoulders. "Don't worry about it," Axel said with a smile. "You'll get it next time."

Silas grunted, but didn't speak. He didn't want to talk to Axel right now. It seemed like Axel always did the right thing, and Silas had just made a huge mistake in front of everybody. He just knew that Finley was going to tease him about it in class.

"Come on, bro. It's all right," Axel tried to say.

"Whatever," Silas grumbled. He knocked Axel's arm off his shoulder as

they walked inside. "We're gonna be late if we don't hurry."

Axel nodded. "Let's get going."

The two boys walked quickly down the hall to their classroom and slid into their seats.

"Psst…"

Silas kept his head down.

"Psst...Silas!" Finley was grinning widely when Silas looked at him.

"What were you dreaming about out there?" Finley laughed. "If it was winning the game, it didn't work."

A few of the other boys snickered and Silas ducked his head. He hated it when he got made fun of. His cheeks always got hot and he stumbled over his words.

"Leave him alone," Axel said in defense. "He just got distracted." Axel glared at Finley, but Silas didn't feel any better.

In fact, having Axel stand up for him made Silas feel worse. He wasn't a little kid who needed someone to speak for them. Biting the inside of his cheek to keep from saying something mean, Silas put his attention on their teacher, Mrs. Whickleby, who was calling the class to attention.

"Today we will break into pairs. Our science project will be volcano lemons."

Silas sat up taller. That sounded cool.

"You and your partner will follow the instructions and write down your observations." Mrs. Whickleby clapped her hands. "Pick a partner and push your desks together."

"Hey, Silas," Axel called out. He waved. "Come over here."

Silas smiled and stood, grabbing his desk in order to push it next to Axel's.

"This is gonna be awesome," Axel said, bouncing in his seat.

Silas nodded. He was still upset about the teasing, but the experiment sounded fun.

"Here's your kit," Mrs. Whickleby said, dropping off a Tupperware container at their desks. "The instructions are inside."

Axel tore open the lid and began pulling everything out. "Here are the instructions." He handed the paper to Silas, who took it and began to read.

"We have to scoop out some of the insides of the lemon." Silas set the paper down and looked at the supplies.

"We can use the spoon," Axel said, grabbing it. He began to attack the lemon with gusto.

"Ow!" Silas covered his eye when a drop of lemon juice squirted his face. "That stuff stings."

"Careful, Mr. Thorsen," Mrs. Whickleby scolded. "We must be gentle or you'll hurt yourself and ruin the experiment."

Silas sunk down in his seat, still rubbing his eye. He glared at Axel, who was too busy working on the lemon to notice. Letting out a huff, Silas folded his arms over his chest and pouted. Today was not turning out to be a good day.

# CHAPTER 3

"All right, everyone!" Mr. Smithfield, the P.E. teacher, rubbed his hands together. "We've been practicing all the different aspects of basketball. Shooting, passing, and dribbling."

Axel bounced on his toes and whispered to Silas, "I'm super excited to play a real game. I love sports."

Silas gave a small smile. He was still a little upset about the experiment in class earlier. But he had to admit that the foam all over the lemon had been pretty cool. Now they were in P.E. and were about to finish their unit on basketball.

"We're going to split into two teams," Mr. Smithfield continued. He looked down at his clipboard. "Emma and Calvin, you'll be the team captains."

The two students walked over to stand by the teacher.

"Emma. Go ahead and pick first. We'll take turns until everyone is on a team." Mr. Smithfield stepped back to wait.

"Axel!" Emma called out quickly.

"Yeah!" Axel pumped a fist in the air and ran over, high-fiving Emma. He stood next to her, grinning widely.

Silas's shoulders fell. He loved basketball and was pretty good at it. Why didn't he get picked first? Last week when they had played P.I.G., Silas had taken second place. But it always seemed to be Axel who was picked first. Ever since he won the soccer game, Axel was picked first for everything.

Silas felt upset. With every student that got picked before him, his fists became tighter and tighter.

At one point, Axel whispered to Emma and they looked at Silas.

"Silas!" she called, waving him over with a smile.

Silas didn't smile back. He felt like a dark cloud was over his head. But he marched to join his team. Then he folded his arms over his chest and scowled. He didn't want to play basketball now. He knew that Axel had told Emma to pick him.

"Great!" Mr. Smithfield said once they were all split up. "Emma, take your team to that basket. Calvin, the other side."

"Hey, Silas!" Axel raised a hand for a high five, but Silas ignored him.

He was still too hurt that he was picked almost last and Axel had been first.

Axel dropped his hand and shrugged. "We're gonna do awesome!" he said, then turned and joined the rest of the team.

Silas walked to his team and tried to be nicer. After all, it wasn't Axel's fault that Emma had picked him first. Taking a deep breath, Silas shoulder-bumped Axel. "Ready to win?" he asked.

Axel's smile came back and he held his hand up again. "You bet!"

Silas high-fived Axel and the game began. Silas tried not to care that Axel got the first basket.

He tried not to point out that every time his team got the ball, they passed it to Axel.

He tried not to notice that Axel stole the ball from the other team four times.

And Silas especially tried not to pay attention when Axel called out that he was open even though Silas had the ball.

Silas dribbled and turned first one way and then the other. Calvin was guarding him, but Silas was taller. He smiled and spun around one more time, trying to fake Calvin out. It worked!

Silas dribbled toward the basket and took a step in order to jump into the air. He threw the ball and watched it sail toward the hoop. It looked like it would be good, but the ball hit the rim and bounced off to the side.

"Ah, man," Axel said. "Better luck next time!"

Before Silas could turn around, Axel was already gone, chasing the other team and trying to keep them from scoring.

All the earlier feelings Silas had struggled with came back. He frowned, not feeling like playing again. Instead, he stood in one spot, even though the

ball and all the other players were down at the opposite basket.

"Watch out!" Axel called.

Silas turned and saw Axel dribbling his way. Silas stepped back just in time for Axel to rush up and put in a lay-up.

Their team cheered and patted Axel on the back.

That heavy cloud was over Silas's head again. Everything was about Axel. Why couldn't Silas be the one to get the basket? Why couldn't his teammates pat him on the back?

"It's just because he's a werewolf," Silas grumbled to himself.

"Isn't Axel great?" Emma asked as she ran past Silas.

Silas's frown grew deeper and he folded his arms over his chest. He was done playing. Huffing, Silas went to sit on the sidelines. He was tired of everything always being about Axel.

# CHAPTER 4

Silas didn't want to go to school the next morning. He was still upset about everything that had happened yesterday.

Why did everything have to be about Axel? Why did Axel have to be so good at sports? And why was Silas feeling like all his friends were leaving him behind in order to be with Axel?

Silas let out a long sigh and played with his bowl of cereal. He put his head in his hand and rested his elbow on the table. Nothing seemed fair at the moment. He just wanted things to go back to the way they were before Axel came to live in their town.

"Let's go!" Sarah called. "We're going to miss the bus."

Silas left his full bowl of cereal on the table and ran to grab his backpack and jacket. The air was still a little bit cold outside, but the sun was bright and made Silas feel slightly better.

"Come on, slow poke!" Sarah shouted. She ran down the driveway and hurried to the group of kids already waiting.

Silas refused to run. He chose to walk because today he didn't care if he missed the bus. He wasn't quite sure what he would do when he got on the bus, since Axel would already be there. Silas wasn't ready to speak to the werewolf yet.

The bright yellow bus pulled up with a screech and puff of smoke.

Coughing, Silas waved away the stinky fog and climbed the steps. Axel was already in a seat, his head poking out the window with his tongue wagging.

Usually, Silas thought Axel's werewolf behavior was funny. But not today.

Silas scowled and sat down by himself across the aisle from Axel, instead of sitting together.

Axel pulled his head inside the bus and frowned. "What's wrong?"

Silas looked out the window and folded his arms over his chest.

Axel jumped across the aisle and sat down next to Silas. "Are you ready for another basketball game today?" he asked in an excited voice. Axel was smiling widely and his sharp teeth gleamed bright in the sunlight.

Silas didn't answer.

Axel nudged his shoulder. "Maybe we can be on the same team

again." He laughed. "That way you'll be on the winning team! We beat those guys good yesterday."

Silas frowned harder.

"Did you like the experiment yesterday? Wasn't that cool when the foam oozed all over our desks?" Axel was getting more and more excited the longer he spoke.

All while Silas was getting more and more angry. He just wanted Axel to leave him alone. Silas's head started to hurt and he closed his eyes, but that only made it so he could hear Axel even better.

"I told them no, I mean, I can't play for the bigger kids or else our team will lose, right?" Axel asked.

Silas shook his head. He didn't know what Axel was talking about, but it didn't matter. It was still all about Axel!

"What do you think we'll do next in P.E.?" Axel began to pant, he was so excited. He reached up and scratched behind his ear. "Now that it's getting warmer, maybe we'll go outside and do races! Do you think we'll do races?" he asked, but he didn't wait for an answer. "Races are so fun! I love chasing cars and I'm really fast. My dad says I'm faster than he was when he was a pup."

The buzzing sound in Silas's head grew louder and louder until Silas thought his head would burst.

"SHUT UP!" he shouted. His mom didn't like him talking to people like that, but right now that didn't matter.

The whole bus grew quiet, but Silas was too angry to care. He turned and pointed a finger at Axel's face. "You're only good at those things because...because...because you're a dog boy!"

Several of the kids gasped and Axel's eyes widened. Dog boy was a name some of the students at their school had called Axel when he'd first arrived. They had been making fun of Axel's behaviors that were more animal than boy.

Silas knew the name had hurt Axel's feelings, but right now Silas was hurting. He was tired of Axel talking about how great he was. He was tired of Axel winning all the games and how all the other kids spoke about him like he was the most important kid on the school grounds.

Just once, Silas wanted to be the best. He wanted to make baskets and have his team cheer instead of groan. He wanted Mrs. Whickleby to say he'd done a good job on his assignment and compliment his work.

Why was being a werewolf so much better than just being Silas?

Axel leaned back, frowning. "What did you call me?"

The bus came to a stop and Silas jumped to his feet. "You heard me," he said. His teeth were clenched. "Just leave me alone."

Shoving past Axel's knees, Silas was the first child off the bus. He didn't wait around for Declan or Axel to get there. Instead, Silas walked straight inside, ignoring all the whispers and murmurs of the other students.

News that he had called Axel a name would spread quickly, and Silas didn't want to wait around. He had thought he and Axel were best friends, but best friends didn't make you feel like you're not important.

Holding his head high, Silas left them all behind. Today was the day he would show them all that he was just as good as Axel Rowe, werewolf or not.

## CHAPTER 5

Silas and Axel didn't speak all morning. When they were asked to gather into pairs for assignments, both of them looked the other way. Silas knew he had hurt Axel's feelings, but Silas's feelings were hurt too!

He was tired of Axel always winning and then telling everyone about it. It was Silas who had gotten the other kids to give Axel a chance, and now Silas was regretting it. It wasn't fun to have one person always be the top dog.

The bell rang, startling Silas. His mind had been wandering all day. A math paper was sitting on his desk and Silas hoped that it made sense. He hadn't been paying attention to what he wrote.

"Lunch time!" Mrs. Whickleby called out with a smile. "Let's head down to the cafeteria."

Silas stood and walked quickly, trying to get away from Axel so he didn't have to stand next to him in line.

"Psssttt…" Emma poked Silas in the back.

Silas looked over his shoulder. "What?"

"How come you and Axel aren't talking to each other?"

Silas scowled. "What's it to you?"

Emma rolled her eyes. "You two are, like, best friends. Why are you so mad?"

A little bit of loneliness crept into Silas's chest and he glanced at Axel. But instead of looking like he was hurting too, Axel was laughing with Henry, another boy in their class. Silas's frown grew deeper. "Things change," he snapped at Emma, then turned around front again.

It wasn't until Silas was putting a hamburger on his tray that she spoke again. "But why?" she hissed. "Axel wins at everything… Why would you be mad at him?"

How could Silas tell her that it was *because* Axel won at everything that they weren't talking? It would sound crazy. It already sounded crazy! It should be awesome that Axel was so good, but it wasn't. It made Silas feel left out and like he wasn't good enough.

"Just because," Silas grumbled at Emma. He didn't want to talk about it. Girls always liked to talk, talk, talk and Silas didn't want to do that. That was part of why he got along with Declan so well. They didn't have to talk to be best friends.

Lifting his tray off the counter edge, Silas turned and looked for his quiet friend. Declan was seated at their usual table, already finishing his peanut butter and jelly sandwich.

"Hey," Silas said, setting his tray down. He stepped over the bench so he could sit.

Declan grunted.

Grabbing a packet of ketchup, Silas let his eyes drift toward the line. Axel had been behind him, so the werewolf should be finishing up about now. Sure enough, Axel had just

stepped away from the counter. His dark eyes met Silas's and the two boys glared at each other.

Silas worried that Axel was going to come over to their table. It would be weird to not talk to each other if they were all sitting together. But Axel stuck his nose in the air and marched in another direction.

Silas watched and his jaw dropped when Axel stopped at the fifth-grade table. Bronson and several of the other boys shouted a greeting to Axel and moved to make a seat for him.

Silas's face warmed and he knew his cheeks were red. It wasn't fair. That was just another slap in the face that Axel was better. Even the older kids liked him.

Declan smacked Silas's arm and mumbled something under his breath.

Silas shook his head. "Nah. Leave him be." He tore off a bite of hamburger, barely tasting it before he swallowed. "If he wants to sit with the big kids, let him. It doesn't mean anything. We don't need him."

Declan stared at Silas, but Silas ignored him.

The boys at the fifth-grade table were laughing hard and Silas couldn't help but wonder what they were talking about. Was Axel telling stories about Silas and Declan?

As the founding members of the HOWL club, the boys had shared almost all of their deepest secrets.

Silas's hand tightened into a fist. Was Axel sharing those secrets? That would go against everything they stood for as a group. It had started because they all admitted they had things about them that were strange. Just like the kids sometimes thought that Axel's werewolf habits were odd. The boys had found through their weirdness, they were actually all the same.

Declan grunted and shrugged before going back to his lunch.

"You're right," Silas said, forcing himself to calm down. "It's probably nothing."

Lunch was eaten in silence as the two friends kept their thoughts to themselves. It was almost like old times, except for the heavy weight that seemed to sit on Silas's shoulders. Instead of being happy that Axel wasn't standing in his way anymore, Silas felt frustrated. He didn't just want Axel to leave him alone, he didn't want Axel to keep winning at all.

Axel wasn't hurt that Silas and he were fighting. Instead, he was sitting with the fifth-graders, getting even more attention than before. Where Silas was getting no attention at all.

He huffed, throwing his lunch back on his tray. "I'm not hungry," he said to Declan. "I'm going out to recess."

# CHAPTER 6

Being outside was helping Silas feel better. He swung across the monkey bars as fast as he could. Out here he didn't have to look at Axel and the older boys laugh and have a good time, while Silas and Declan sat by themselves.

It just wasn't fair. Axel was everyone's favorite. He won at sports and in class. Silas wasn't a bad student. He'd won student of the month last year and usually got along well with his teachers. This year Axel was ruining everything.

Everyone wanted to get to know the school werewolf and Axel was eating it up, instead of being a good friend to Silas and Declan.

Dropping to the ground, Silas wiped his sweaty hands on his shirt and hurried over to where Declan was playing a game with his cards.

"Who's winning?" Silas asked.

Declan made some noises and Silas nodded.

"Huh. I thought Mega Gengar was better than Mega Venusaur."

Declan shook his head and huffed.

"I'll have to remember that for next time," Silas said. He looked around. His eyes landed on a large group of boys coming out from lunch. Axel was right in the middle and looked like he was happy as a clam. Silas scowled.

"Silas!" Emma shouted, waving her hand at him. "We're gonna start a game. Come on."

Silas took a step in their direction, then stopped. He wasn't sure if he wanted to go play. Axel would be there and that would ruin everything. Again.

"He's probably playing for the fifth-graders," Silas grumbled.

Declan snorted and Silas turned around.

"I don't want to play with him, all right? There's nothing wrong with that," Silas defended himself.

Declan looked up at Silas, then went back to his game.

"Come on, Si!" Emma shouted right before she took off running.

Silas sighed and started walking. He really didn't want to go, but he didn't know how to tell Emma and the other kids on his team that. He stayed at the back of the group as they started to assign positions on the field.

"Take goalie," Finley said to Silas, pointing toward the goal.

Silas scowled, but went over like he'd been told. At least as goalie, he wouldn't have to deal with Axel very much.

The game went on for several minutes before the ball started coming in Silas's direction. He crouched down and held his arms out to the side. The fifth-grader who was dribbling kicked the ball off to a teammate. Then Silas realized that Axel was just to his left.

Axel caught the ball with his foot and shifted quickly. He began coming toward Silas.

Silas held his breath. Axel was really fast. It was hard to keep up with him. Even Finley couldn't stop the werewolf.

Deep determination began to build inside Silas. He was desperate for a chance to beat Axel at something...*anything!* Right now was his chance. Silas knew that Axel wouldn't pass the ball to anyone else.

If Silas could stop the goal, then he'd have won. It wouldn't stop the game, but it would still be a victory against Axel. And that's exactly what Silas wanted.

He focused on the ball, watching it bounce on the ground and between Axel's quick feet. Silas had never felt so focused before. The rest of the team disappeared. Silas found himself mesmerized by the ball, his body automatically moving wherever the ball went.

Finally Axel got close enough for a shot. His leg went back, almost in slow motion, and he kicked the ball hard.

Silas's eyes grew wide as he threw himself into the air toward the ball. He just knew he was going to stop it. He was going to win! He flew sideways through the air, his hands stretched out as far as they would go. The ball hit his fingers, bending them backwards as it continued into the net.

Reality hit Silas in the face as he landed hard on the short grass. His breath whooshed out of him as he landed. Silas lay on the ground, his chest and hip hurting from the fall. Inside, his heart also ached because he had failed.

He'd tried so hard, given it everything he had, and Silas still didn't win.

"Come on, Si!" Finley shouted. "Get up!"

Silas slowly climbed to his feet. As he brushed the grass off his shirt, a hand came into his vision.

"Nice try," Axel said, holding out a fist.

Silas scowled at his ex-friend. "Go away."

Axel's thick eyebrows pointed down. "I was trying to be nice."

"Whatever!" Silas shouted. "Just go away! This is all your fault!"

"All my fault?" Axel shouted back. "It's my fault that you're not as good as me?"

Silas jerked back. Axel's words might be true, but they made the wound inside Silas hurt more than ever.

"I thought friends didn't care about things like that," Axel said with a growl.

"Friends might," Silas said. He put his nose in the air and began to walk away. "Good thing we're not friends."

# CHAPTER 7

Silas stood in the lunch room holding his lunch with a shaking hand. He looked around for a place to sit. Axel was sitting with the older kids. He was completely ignoring Silas. Silas grit his teeth. Who cared? He didn't want to sit with a stinky werewolf anyway.

Silas looked around for Declan and found him sitting with Finley and the other fourth-graders. Silas took a step in their direction. Finley looked up and spotted him, then turned and whispered behind his hand. Soon the whole table was looking at Silas and laughing behind their hands. All except Declan. He wasn't laughing, but he wasn't standing up to be with Silas either.

A strange emptiness sunk into Silas's stomach. Suddenly he wasn't hungry. At all. He turned to leave, but a teacher was standing in the doorway, blocking the kids from walking out. With a huff, Silas went to the far corner and sat down.

His lunch bag sat on the table uneaten as the other students ate and laughed with each other. The noise became a blur as Silas grew sadder and sadder. He blinked several times. He didn't want to cry. If the other boys saw that, they would only make fun of him even more.

It wasn't fair!

Everybody loved Axel. He got all the attention. He was good at everything. He always won. Why did Axel get everything and Silas got nothing?

Silas scowled and folded his arms over his chest. "I wish he hadn't moved here," Silas grumbled to himself.

He glanced up to see the other kids starting to leave the tables. Finally, he could go outside. Maybe everything would be okay when they started the soccer game. Maybe Silas would block a goal and redeem himself from yesterday.

Silas threw his lunch in the garbage and marched outside with his head high. He didn't want anyone to know how much his heart hurt. He was fine. He wasn't the one being mean. Axel was mean. Finley was mean. Declan was mean. They were all against Silas and it wasn't Silas's fault!

A few kids had gathered on the soccer field when Silas walked across the grass.

"Want me to play goalie?" Silas asked. He started to walk toward the goal.

"Hey, Silas," Emma said, waving him over.

Silas jogged to her side. "What?"

Emma looked embarrassed as she looked at the grass. "We, uh, we don't need you to play goalie today."

Silas paused. "What?"

Emma couldn't seem to meet his eyes. "We have someone else playing goalie."

The pain in Silas's heart began to hurt even more. He put his hands on his hips. "Who?" he demanded.

Emma shrugged. "I don't know. Finley said he had someone."

"Let's play!" Finley shouted as he and the other fourth-grade boys ran across the grass to the soccer field.

"Finley!" Silas waved his hand to get the other student's attention.

Finley stopped and looked back over his shoulder. "What do *you* want?" Finley said with a sneer.

Silas almost walked away. Finley could be really rude sometimes and Silas didn't like to fight. But instead, he reminded himself that the fight with Axel wasn't his fault. "Emma said you don't want me to play goalie."

Finley folded his arms. "That's right. We have someone else."

"I want to know who," Silas said.

Finley shrugged. "Doesn't matter. We don't need you anymore." Finley turned around and left before Silas could say anything else.

The other kids gave Silas sad looks before leaving him alone on the sidelines. For a few minutes, Silas didn't move. The other kids began to play. The soccer ball moved up and down the field. Most of the time, Finley or Axel had it. Neither one of them paid any attention to Silas.

Feeling sick to his stomach, Silas turned and walked away. He went to the monkey bars and climbed up to the top. He didn't want to talk to anybody right now. He had never felt so sad and so lonely. Why couldn't anyone see that Silas just wanted to win for once? He just wanted to be good at something?

While he was fighting back tears, the bell rang and Silas jumped in shock. He grabbed the bars to keep from falling off. Then he started to climb down. His head hung low as he walked inside. All the other kids were shouting and having fun. But Silas was all alone.

It felt like nobody cared. Everyone had chosen to stay friends with Axel instead of Silas. This wasn't how it was supposed to be. Declan was supposed to stay friends with Silas. He should have understood why Silas was upset.

Once in his seat, Mrs. Whickleby began to talk, but Silas didn't hear any of it. He couldn't get past how lonely he was feeling. Right now he was in a classroom with twenty other kids and he still felt alone.

Axel was sitting to Silas's right. He ignored Silas completely. It was as if Silas didn't even exist. It made Silas wonder... If he left school, would the teacher know? Would anyone care?

He began to doodle on his notebook. He liked to doodle, but right now it didn't make him feel better. All of a sudden, Silas's stomach growled.

The whole class heard it and several kids turned around to see who it was.

Silas's cheeks felt hot as he grew embarrassed. He slumped in his seat, trying to hide. Apparently, he wasn't as invisible as he thought because the other kids pointed their fingers and laughed at him again.

"Children!" Mrs. Whickleby clapped her hands. It took a moment, but the class finally quieted down. "We do not laugh at each other," she said sternly. "Our job is to help each other feel good, not hurt each other's feelings." She looked over her glasses at Silas. "Did you get enough to eat at lunch, Silas?"

He didn't want everyone to know he'd thrown his lunch away. They would just make fun of him again. "Yeah," he muttered, sinking even lower in his seat.

"Well, I suppose you're just a growing boy, then," Mrs. Whickleby said with a smile. She winked at him, then turned around and started writing on the whiteboard.

This was officially the worst day of school ever. Silas wished he could disappear for real.

# **CHAPTER 8**

Silas didn't eat much dinner that night. Even though he'd skipped lunch, his stomach wouldn't stop churning. The situation at school was ruining his entire life.

"Mom?" he asked after dinner.

"Yes, Silas?" she answered from the sink. His mom was doing dishes.

"Can I go speak to Declan for a minute?"

"Mm, hm," she hummed absent-mindedly.

Silas left the house quickly, before she could change her mind. His walking slowed as he approached Declan's house. Declan hadn't talked to Silas today either. *Maybe he won't want to see me.* But Silas was out of ideas. He needed to talk to someone who would understand. Maybe if Silas explained everything to Declan, Declan would be his friend again.

Silas knocked and Mrs. Murray answered the door. "Hello, Silas. How are you today?"

"Fine, thanks," Silas said. He kept his eyes on his shoes. "Is Declan home?"

"Uh, huh," Mrs. Murray said with a kind smile. "Come on in."

Silas shuffled inside, feeling more nervous with every step. He was really worried Declan wouldn't walk to talk to him, but if ever Silas needed a friend...it was now.

"He's in his room," Mrs. Murray said. "Go ahead." She waved a hand down the hall.

Silas swallowed hard. He knew where Declan's room was. He'd been here many times before. "Thanks," Silas said softly before walking to Declan's door. His hand was shaking a little, but Silas forced himself to knock.

Declan grunted and Silas slowly pushed the door open.

Declan looked up from his seat on the floor. His cards were all laid out in front of him. His black eyebrows rose up high on his forehead.

Silas shrugged and stuffed his hands in his pockets. "Hey."

Declan gave Silas a chin tilt, then looked back down.

Silas sighed in relief. He was so glad Declan wasn't mad. Walking over, he sat on the other side of the cards. "Can I talk to you for a minute?"

Delcan mumbled.

Silas picked at the carpet. "I don't know what to do," he started. He paused for a split second, then the entire story came pouring out. It seemed the more Silas talked, the more he needed to talk.

Declan listened the whole time, only making a few noises to let Silas know he was still paying attention.

Silas was breathing heavily when he was done with his story. He felt much better now that he'd shared his troubles with a friend. It made him wonder if that's why girls talk so much. Maybe it helped them feel better too. "So...what do you think?"

Declan didn't say anything for a long time. Finally he put down his cards and made a face.

Silas sighed. "I know," he admitted. "I shouldn't have said those things."

Declan grumbled, then went back to his cards.

"But Axel shouldn't have said those things either!" Silas defended himself.

Declan looked up and shrugged.

Silas groaned and let himself fall back on the carpet. "You're right. But it's still hard. But Mom always said that being unkind to unkind people never helped anybody."

Declan nodded.

"Okay...so Axel isn't *unkind*, but he still brags a lot." Silas lifted his head to look at Declan. "And that hurts when he's always reminding me how much better he is."

Declan spread out three cards.

"Yes, I remember he's a werewolf," Silas said sarcastically. "Of course he's going to be good at what he does. But that doesn't mean he has to be rude about it."

Declan turned over another card.

Silas let his head fall back. "Okay, okay. I'll apologize tomorrow. Happy?"

Declan gave him a small grin and Silas was glad for it. Everything Declan said had already been in Silas's mind, but he needed his friend to remind him of what was right. Silas has been so hurt and angry that he'd forgotten that he needed to make good choices too.

Declan made another noise and Silas frowned.

"I'd forgotten that," Silas said softly. He smiled. "You know...that's a good idea. Maybe now is a good time to get started." He paused. "If my mom says yes anyway."

Declan shuffled his cards.

"Thanks, man," Silas said sincerely. He and Declan had been friends a long time. He might be a little different than the other boys, but that's part of what made him such a good friend. Silas held out his hand and the two of them did a fun handshake they'd made up when they were little boys.

When they were done, Declan grabbed a stack of cards and handed them to Silas.

Silas raised his eyebrows. "You sure you want me to play? I'm terrible."

When Declan grinned, Silas laughed.

"Maybe I'll beat you, just this once," Silas teased. Still smiling, he settled down to play with Declan, their fight long forgotten.

Silas knew, though, that tomorrow would come quickly. And when it did, he had a tough job ahead. It wasn't easy to apologize, but hopefully, it would help all of them feel better in the end.

## CHAPTER 9

Silas climbed the bus steps slowly the next morning. He knew Declan was right. He needed to apologize. But that didn't make it easy. He kept his eyes down as he walked between the seats. He knew Axel would already be on the bus, but he wouldn't be saving a seat like he normally did. They hadn't sat together in over a week.

Silas jerked to a stop when he heard a loud grunt. Looking up, he saw Declan. Declan smiled and jerked his head, telling Silas to come over by him.

Silas walked to Declan's seat. "Are you sure you want me to sit here?"

Declan huffed and grunted, then scooted closer to the window.

Silas smiled and sat down. Once again he was grateful for his friend. "Thanks."

Declan grinned again. His eyes went to the seat behind them and Silas stiffened. He knew that Axel would be in that seat.

Slowly, Silas turned around. Axel was up on his knees, his hands on the window, staring. His head wasn't hanging out like usual. And his tongue stayed in his mouth. It was unusual for

Axel to not enjoy the smells on the way to school. He always said things smelled better in the morning.

"Hey," Silas said softly. He wasn't sure if Axel would talk to him, but he'd promised Declan he'd try.

Axel looked over, then scowled. He turned back to the window.

"Axel?" Silas asked.

Axel rolled his eyes. "What?" he snapped.

"I'm sorry," Silas said.

Axel froze, then slowly turned to look at Silas. "What?" he asked.

Silas swallowed hard. It felt like someone had punched him in the stomach, he was so nervous. "I'm sorry."

Axel said down on the seat, then scooted to the edge so he could see Silas better. "You're sorry, huh?" Axel folded his arms over his chest. "For what?"

Silas hung his head and looked down at the ground. Declan nudged his arm and Silas nodded. He knew what Declan wanted him to do. "I'm sorry I was jealous."

Axel's arms fell to the side. "You were jealous?"

Silas nodded. "Yeah."

"About what?" Axel asked in surprise. His eyes were wide and his mouth open as he stared at Silas.

"About...everything!" Silas said. He waved a hand in the air as he talked. "You're so good at sports. All the older kids want to be your friend. You get picked by our teacher for everything! I mean, everything you do, you're the best at!" Silas pouted. "I just wanted to be good at something too. But then you were still better."

Axel's eyes grew even wider. "Ooooh. You mean when we played basketball."

Silas nodded miserably. It hurt to apologize, but it also hurt to talk about his failures. It was no wonder Axel didn't want to be his friend. Silas wouldn't be his own friend in real life! Silas's head jerked up when Axel punched him in the shoulder.

"Dude! You don't fail at everything! You're awesome!" Axel was grinning widely, showing off his sharp teeth.

"No, I'm not," Silas argued. "You were better than me at basketball. I can't stop the ball in soccer to save my life. You run faster. You're stronger."

Silas rolled his eyes. "You even have better hair!"

Axel laughed and Declan snorted. "But what about you?" Axel demanded.

"What about me?" Silas asked.

"You're better at some things," Axel insisted.

"Oh yeah? Like what?" Silas asked.

"Like at making friends," Axel said. "You weren't afraid to talk to me even though everyone else was."

Silas shrugged. "So what?"

"And you won the spelling bee last month," Axel reminded him.

"I guess I am kinda good at spelling," Silas said slowly.

"And you bring the best snacks when we have HOWL Club."

Silas grinned. "That's because of my mom, not me."

Axel shook his head. "Maybe so, but you don't have to share them."

"Thanks," Silas said. He was starting to feel better. Axel and Declan were talking to him and it sounded like Axel had kind of felt the same way about Silas that Silas felt about Axel.

"We werewolves *are* good at sports," Axel boasted. "But there are other things to be good at." He puffed up his chest, but stopped when he saw Silas looking sad again. "What's wrong?"

Silas pinched his lips together. He wasn't sure how to tell Axel that those kinds of words hurt his feelings.

Declan grunted and grumbled.

Axel's ears perked up and he looked back at Silas. "Was I bragging?"

Silas scrunched up his nose. "Kinda, yeah."

Axel scratched his ear. "I'm sorry. I don't mean to." He leaned in closer. "My mom says I do that sometimes and it doesn't make people feel good."

Silas nodded. "She's right."

Axel's shoulders slumped. "Sorry."

"Me too," Silas responded.

Axel sat up and held out his fist. "Think we can be friends again?"

A slow smile crept across Silas's face. "Really?"

Axel shook his head. "Hey, don't leave me hanging!"

Silas laughed and fist-bumped Axel. "That'd be great."

"The HOWL Club is officially back in action!" Axel punched a fist in the air, then slammed into the seat in front of him when the bus stopped. "Oops," he said, laughing.

Silas laughed with him and together, they all walked off the bus.

"Hey, Dog Boy!" One of the fifth-graders waved at Axel, calling him over to their group.

Axel took a step then stopped and looked back at Silas. He smiled, then turned to the other boy. "Sorry! I'm with my friends today!"

Silas smiled when Axel put his arm around Silas's shoulders and they walked inside.

## CHAPTER 10

"I hereby bring the HOWL Club meeting to order!" Silas called, hitting a brick with a hammer.

Axel shifted in his seat, waving his hand wildly in the air.

Silas rolled his eyes. "We just got started," he whined.

Axel just waved his hand harder.

"What is it?" Silas asked.

I've got an announcement," Axel said with a grin.

Silas waited, but Axel didn't say anything else.

Declan grunted and Silas grinned.

Axel was still bouncing in his seat. "I got onto the league soccer team."

Silas smiled wide. He found that he really was happy for his friend. Axel really was good at soccer and it was okay for him to be able to play with the older kids. "Congrats!" he said. He stepped over the brick and gave the werewolf a high five.

Declan held out his fist and Axel bumped it with his own.

"Thanks, guys!" Axel gushed. His sharp teeth were showing from his big smile. "I'm really excited." He quieted down a little. "But I'm a little nervous too."

Silas shrugged. "You're awesome. You're the best soccer player I've ever seen, so don't be nervous." He pretended to kick a soccer ball. "You'll race circles around the older kids."

Axel laughed. "I hope so."

"I know so," Silas encouraged. He sat down on the floor with the other boys. "Anything else we need to talk about?"

Axel scrunched his lips to the side. He looked at Declan. "You got anything?"

Declan shook his head and made a humming sound. He pulled a pack of Pokemon cards out of his pocket and began to organize them on the treehouse floor.

Axel looked back to Silas and asked, "What about you?"

Silas scratched his head. "I don't know." His eyes got wide. "Oh. I'm starting something new next week." Declan had reminded Silas he'd wanted to do this for a long time. Now seemed like a good time to start.

"Really? What?" Axel asked.

Declan looked up from his cards and waited.

"Well…" Silas rubbed the back of his neck. He was a little nervous about sharing with Axel. He had never done anything like this before, but secretly Silas was excited.

"Come on," Axel urged. "I told you about my soccer tryouts. They were really crazy, and look how it turned out!"

Silas nodded. "It's just...different." He had always played sports at school, like most of the other boys. Silas still really liked sports, but after his talk with Declan, he had realized that maybe he had talents that were a little different. After talking to his mom, Silas had decided to try something new.

"Just tell us!" Axel practically shouted. He was bouncing in his seat again.

"I'm going to take guitar lessons," Silas said softly.

Axel's jaw dropped open and his ears twitched. "Whoa...really?"

Declan grumbled under his breath.

Silas shrugged. "I'm playing acoustic guitar. You know...the wooden kind? But I think I'd like to learn electric guitar someday too."

"Dude!" Axel shouted. "You're gonna be a rockstar!"

All of Silas's worries melted away. It didn't matter that he was interested in something different than his friends. They liked him for who he was and were happy for him, just like Silas was happy for Axel and his soccer playing.

"Thanks," he said. His cheeks felt hot as Axel began to dance around the treehouse playing an air guitar.

"Soccer, music, and Pokemon?" Axel laughed. "Dude, we're awesome. We do EVERYTHING!"

Silas laughed at his friend's enthusiasm. When Axel let out a loud howl, all of the boys began to laugh, rolling around on the ground.

Silas felt happier than he had in a long time. He was eager to learn something new, and he was also excited to support his friends in their own activities. Right now...life was pretty darn good.

## THANK YOU!

If you enjoyed this book please leave a review on your favorite retailer! Reviews are a great way to support your favorite authors and help others find their books.

Don't miss Silas, Axel and Declan in

"The Werewolf Makes a Goal"

Book #3 in the

'There's a Werewolf in my School' series.

Made in the USA
Las Vegas, NV
07 September 2021